Contents

Our Colourful Language 2

Blue 4

Green 10

Yellow 16

Red 22

White 28

Black 34

Colourful Crossword 40

Crossword Clues 42

What Is It? – Answers 44

Index 46

To Thomas, Katherine, and Benjamin, whose lives are full of colour

Our Colourful

Colour is an important feature of the world we live in. It is also an important feature of language. Have you ever thought about all the words and phrases in the English language that begin with a colour? Some of them, such as *blueberry*, have straightforward meanings. A blueberry is a berry that is blue. Other words and phrases are more complex. For example, *white horses* can refer to horses that are white, but the phrase can also be used to describe white-capped waves rolling in from the sea!

Colour words can have several meanings. The word *blue* refers to a colour, an emotion, a family of butterflies, and a powder used to whiten laundry!

Language

So, is a bluebottle a blue-coloured bottle, or is it something else? And what is a yellowlegs? To know more about our language, we need to know where words and phrases come from, and what they mean, exactly.

Blue

Bluebird
The bluebird is one of North America's few songbirds. It is a member of the thrush family, and gets its name from its deep blue plumage.

There are several other birds with the colour blue in their names. Among them are the blue throat, which is also related to the thrush; an Asian bird known as a fairy bluebird; a pigeon named the blue rock; the blue jay from North America and Canada; and a tiny bird named the blue tit, which is found in most parts of the world.

Blue Whale

The blue whale is an incredibly large animal. It can grow to be more than 30-metres long and weigh 130 tonnes, which is the weight of about 35 full-grown elephants. It is bigger than any dinosaur that ever lived! Like all whales, the blue whale is a mammal, giving birth to live young and feeding them milk. But because of its huge size, the blue whale has to live in the sea. If whales are stranded on land, their immense body weight can crush their internal organs. The buoyancy of the sea prevents this from happening.

Blue Ribbon

A blue-ribbon event is the top event in a particular sport or competition. The World Cup is the blue-ribbon event of several international sports, for example, soccer, rugby, and skiing. The Olympic Games is athletics' blue-ribbon event, and the America's Cup is a blue-ribbon event of yachting.

This term comes from the highest order of knighthood in the British Commonwealth.

The Noble Order of the Garter dates back to 1348, and its emblem is a blue ribbon worn on the leg by men and on the arm by women.

Blue Peter

The Blue Peter is a blue flag with a white panel at its centre. It is flown by ships in harbour on the day they are leaving port. It warns passengers and crew that they should be on board.

Bluebottle

Bluebottle is the name given to a large fly with a blue body.

A bluebottle is also a Portuguese man-of-war. Although it resembles a jellyfish, the Portuguese man-of-war is a large colony of jellyfish-like creatures, which can survive only when they exist together.

BLUE SAYINGS AND PHRASES

To look or feel blue – to look or feel sad

To be blue in the face – to have tried very hard; to be breathless and exhausted, either physically or mentally

Once in a blue moon – this refers to something that happens rarely. Very occasionally, the moon may appear to be blue, because of dust in the atmosphere from major volcanic eruptions, or very large forest fires.

Blues – a traditional form of African-American music. Blues songs are often sad, but some take a humorous or defiant stand against life's troubles.

Blue

(adj.) 1. having the colour blue, like a clear sky or the deep sea **2.** feeling sad, depressed **3.** having bluish skin through cold, fear, anger, etc. **(n.) 1.** the colour blue **2.** a particular family of butterflies **3.** a powder used to whiten laundry

WHAT IS IT?

A *bluegum* is:
1. Blue bubblegum
2. Blue glue
3. Gum disease
4. A eucalyptus tree native to Australia

Green

Greenhouse

A greenhouse is a building made of glass or plastic in which plants are grown. Greenhouses catch and hold heat from the sun, so they are used to shelter plants that need a warm climate. It is easier to keep pests away from plants growing in a greenhouse. Often, however, insects such as greenhouse grasshoppers get in, stay hidden during the day, and feed on the plants during the night.

Greenhouse Effect

When people talk about the greenhouse effect, they are referring to the way Earth's surface is being heated up as a result of too much carbon dioxide in the atmosphere. Carbon dioxide is produced by burning coal and other fossil fuels, car fumes, some aerosols, and industrial pollution. The destruction of forests, which absorb carbon dioxide, is also contributing to the greenhouse effect. Carbon dioxide traps warmth from the sun in the same way a greenhouse does, causing Earth's surface to heat.

Green Tree Python

Green tree pythons live in Northern Australia and New Guinea. They are green snakes with white spots along their backs. Their colouring makes them difficult to see among leaves. They change, or shed, their skins about once every six weeks.

Green Tree Frog

Most green tree frogs are less than 5-centimetres long. They can be found on all continents except Antarctica. Like the green tree python, the colour of the green tree frog allows it to hide from enemies and prey.

Greenland

Greenland is a large island in the Arctic that is actually part of the Danish Kingdom. A Viking explorer named Eric the Red claimed to have discovered Greenland in 982. He named the island Greenland in an attempt to attract settlers. But the coastal areas of Greenland become green only during the summer. Most of the island is covered in ice year-round.

GREEN SAYINGS AND PHRASES

The green-eyed monster – William Shakespeare (1564-1616), a famous playwright and poet, called jealousy the green-eyed monster. In the past, someone with a greenish complexion was thought to be jealous.

To get the green light – to get permission to go ahead with a project

Greenhorn – an inexperienced or foolish person. This word comes from the "green horns" of a young, horned animal.

The grass is always greener on the other side of the fence – a proverb meaning that what you don't have may appear to be better than what you do have

Green

(adj.) 1. having the colour green, like grass **2.** inexperienced or immature **3.** concerned about nature and the environment **4.** unripe or unseasoned **5.** not dried, smoked, or tanned **6.** (of the complexion) **a.** pale, sickly looking **b.** jealous, envious **(n.) 1.** the colour green **2.** an area of grass-covered land in the centre of town (the village green) **3.** an area of short grass either on a bowling-green or putting-green of a golf course **4. greens** – green vegetables

WHAT IS IT?

A *green thumb* is:
1. A type of tree
2. Something a person is said to have if they are good at growing plants
3. A greenish thumb
4. Tom Thumb's first cousin

Yellow

Yellowstone Park

The oldest national park in the world, Yellowstone National Park was established in 1872 and is the largest national park in the United States. It is situated in the north-west of Wyoming and spreads into Idaho and Montana. It was named after the yellow rocks of the Yellowstone River, which lies north of the park.

Yellowstone National Park contains more geysers and hot springs than any other area in the world. It is also the largest wildlife reserve in the United States.

The park is home to more than 200 types of birds and 40 types of animals, including bears, elk, moose, bison, bald eagles, trumpeter swans, and white pelicans. Over 2 million people visit the park every year.

Yellow Jacket

A yellow jacket is a small wasp with black-and-yellow markings which act as a warning to birds and other insect-eating animals to keep away. Yellow jackets build their nests using paper which they make by chewing rotten wood. Nests are often found underground, hanging in trees, inside tree stumps, or within the walls of buildings. A yellow jacket community is highly organized, with female workers and males serving their queen. Only the females are able to sting and will do so repeatedly to defend their nest.

Yellow River

The Yellow River is the second-longest river in China. The Chinese name for the river is Huang He, but it is widely known as the Yellow River because, as it flows across China, it picks up a great deal of yellow silt that makes its waters turn yellow. The Yellow River often overflows, causing terrible floods. Large dams have now been built along the river, not only to produce electricity, but also to store water for use in times of drought.

Yellow-Eyed Penguin

Yellow-eyed penguins get their name primarily because they have yellow eyes, but also because they have bands of yellow feathers encircling their heads. The penguins do not develop this colouring until they are about fifteen months old.

The yellow-eyed penguin is an endangered species and can be found only in New Zealand. The penguins live on the south-east coast of the South Island, Stewart Island, and on some subantarctic islands. Many people are trying to preserve the penguins' coastal habitats and provide new nesting sites, hoping to increase the population of yellow-eyed penguins.

YELLOW SAYINGS AND PHRASES

Yellow, yellow-livered, yellow belly – a coward

Yellow ribbon – Tying a yellow ribbon around a tree if a family member or friend is a prisoner of war or missing for some other reason shows that the person is not forgotten. The ribbon remains tied around the tree until the person returns home.

Yellow fever – a tropical fever accompanied by jaundice and vomiting, also called yellow jack. In countries where gold was discovered in the past, the gold-mining mania was sometimes referred to as yellow fever.

Yellow flag – a flag displayed by a ship in quarantine

Yellow

(adj.) 1. having the colour yellow, like a lemon or egg-yolk **2.** having a yellow complexion **3.** cowardly **(n.)** the colour yellow **(v.) 1.** to make or become yellow or yellowish (The newspaper had *yellowed* with age.)

WHAT IS IT?

A *yellowlegs* is:
1. A person who runs when faced with danger
2. An American shorebird
3. A person wearing yellow stockings or trousers
4. A French dish similar to frogs' legs

Red

Red Crab

There are said to be about 120 million red crabs living in the rainforest on Christmas Island, in the Indian Ocean. In November, when the rainy season begins, the crabs leave the forest and march towards the sea to breed. They swarm across railway lines and roads, often halting traffic. When they reach the beach, the crabs mate, and each female leaves about 100,000 eggs in the sea, before returning to the forest. Once the red crabs hatch, they instinctively make their way inland. Thousands are eaten by other crabs and birds, but most survive the journey back to the rainforest.

Redwood

Redwoods are among the tallest trees in the world. They commonly grow up to 90-metres high and 4-6 metres in diameter. They can live for 2,000 years. Redwoods, named because their wood is red, grow along the West Coast of the United States, from central California to southern Oregon. The tallest known living tree in the world is a redwood in northern California. It is about 112-metres high.

Red Cross

The Red Cross is an organization that attempts to relieve human suffering. Red Cross workers provide aid in times of war or peace and serve people of all races, nationalities, and religions. Following a disaster, the Red Cross provides medical attention, food and water, shelter, blankets, and clothing.

Red Cross societies are found in more than 135 countries. The Red Cross flag is a red cross on a white background. This flag was chosen because the Red Cross was founded in Switzerland, in 1863, and the Swiss flag is a white cross on a red background.

Societies in most Muslim countries use a red crescent on a white background, and in Israel the symbol is a red Star of David on a white background.

Red Planet

The planet Mars is often called the red planet because it appears reddish. It was named after Mars, the Roman god of war. It is the fourth planet from the sun – Earth is the third. Mars is a little over half the size of Earth. Its surface is more like Earth's surface than any other planet. However, the plants and animals of Earth could not survive on Mars.

RED SAYINGS AND PHRASES

Red tape – a term used to describe the inefficiency of large companies, governments, or official routine in general. This expression came from England during the 1700s, when many officials tied their documents together with red tape.

Red carpet – a term referring to special treatment given to an important visitor

Red sky at night, shepherd's delight
Red sky in the morning, shepherd's warning – this is an old saying used to forecast the weather. Supposedly, if there is a red sunset, a fine day will follow. But if there is a red sunrise, rain can be expected during the day.

In the red – to be overdrawn at the bank, or in debt. This comes from the business practice of showing overdrawn accounts in red ink.

Red
(adj.) 1. having the colour red, like blood or cherries **2.** flushed in the face with shame, anger, etc. **3.** (of the eyes) bloodshot or red-rimmed from weeping **(n.) 1.** the colour red

WHAT IS IT?

A *red-letter day* is:
1. A day when everybody must write with a red pen or pencil
2. Another name for Valentine's Day
3. A lucky, noteworthy, or memorable day
4. A day when posties dress in red

White

White House

The White House is the official residence of the president of the United States. It is situated in Washington, DC, the capital of the United States. The 132-room White House contains numerous offices and huge reception rooms for official social functions. The original building was begun in 1792, but was destroyed by fire in 1814. A new building was erected using white limestone and became widely known as the White House. In 1901, President Roosevelt authorized "White House" as the building's official title.

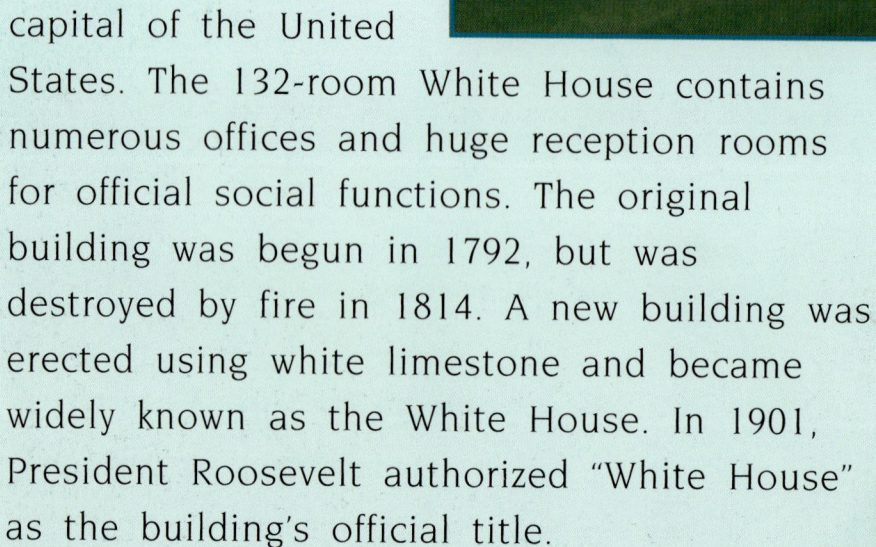

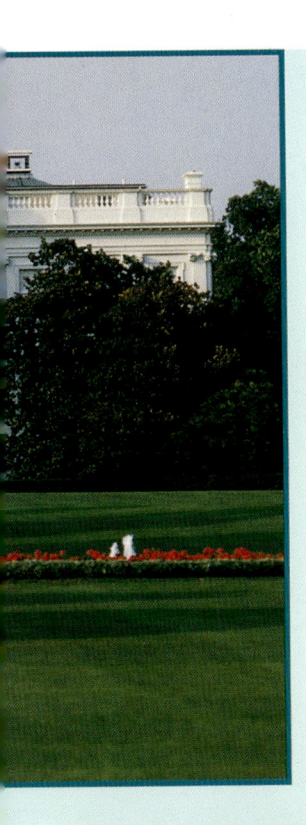

White-Out

A white-out is an atmospheric condition in which low clouds or mist blankets the slopes of a mountain. During a white-out, it is difficult to distinguish where the ground ends and the sky begins. It's even difficult to see a large object such as a helicopter! Skiing in such conditions can be very dangerous. A good pair of goggles or sunglasses may make it a little easier to see.

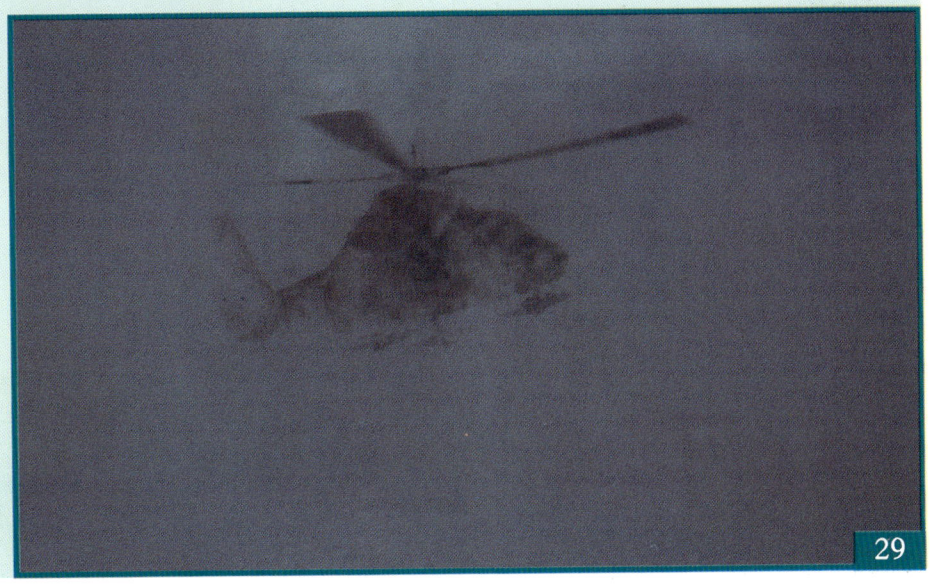

White Rhinoceros

Underneath the dust, both white and black rhinoceros are the same dull bluish-grey colour, but they have been given their names, white and black, from the colour of the dust or mud in which they roll. More accurate names for these animals would be the square-lipped rhinoceros for the white and the hook-lipped rhinoceros for the black. Both species live in Africa, where the white rhinoceros is a grazer, eating grass, and the black is a browser, eating leaves and twigs. The white rhinoceros was once nearly extinct, and few remain in the wild.

White Water

The term *white water* refers to fast-flowing water that is churned up and topped with white foam. White-water rafting is a popular, exciting, and sometimes dangerous, sport. The rafters use a flexible rubber raft – with ropes around the outside for hand-holds – and paddles to make their way down the river. Everyone must wear helmets and life jackets in case the raft is overturned or they are thrown out.

WHITE SAYINGS AND PHRASES

White elephant – a useless and troublesome possession or thing. This phrase dates back to when the King of Siam (now named Thailand) used to present a white elephant to an official that he did not like. The white elephant would be difficult to look after and keep clean, causing the owner enormous expense. However, the gift would have to be kept so as not to upset the king.

White-collar worker – a professional or clerical worker. Such people often wear white shirts.

White-tie affair – a social function at which men wear full evening dress with white bow ties and women wear long evening dresses or formal trouser suits

To *hit the white* – to be correct, or make a good shot. This phrase comes from archery where the inner circle of the target is white.

White
(adj.) 1. having the colour white, like snow or milk (Although we refer to white as a colour, it is really the combination of all colours. Something appears to be white when it reflects all the light rays that make colour.) **2.** having a pale colour (*white* meat of a turkey) **3.** (of tea or coffee) served with milk or cream **(n.) 1.** the colour white **2. *whites*** – white garments worn in sports such as cricket or tennis

WHAT IS IT?

A *white night* is:
1. A snowy night
2. A night on which the moon shines so brightly that indoor lighting is not needed
3. A sleepless night
4. A good knight

Black

North American Black Bear

Black bears are the most common, and also the smallest, bears in North America. They can be found in Alaska, Canada, and the United States. They are called black bears because most of them are black. However, some have brown noses, white patches on their chest, or a rusty-brown coat. North American black bears grow to about 1.5-metres tall.

Blacksmith

A blacksmith is a person who works with iron, a black metal. The iron is heated in the forge until it is red-hot and malleable. The blacksmith then holds the hot iron with a pair of metal tongs and hammers it into shape on an anvil. After shaping the metal, the blacksmith plunges it into cold water so that it quickly cools and hardens, keeping its new shape. Many things can be made using this method, from household tools to gates. In the past, horseshoes were perhaps the most important item a blacksmith made. With today's modern machinery and mass-production methods, blacksmiths have become few and far between. However, some people still have the skills and like to work with traditional methods.

Black Widow Spider

The female black widow is very dangerous. Its bite can cause severe pain and illness. The black widow got its name because the female sometimes kills the male after mating. For this reason, the female black widow is seen more often than the male. The female black widow has a shiny black body with a red or yellow mark in the shape of an hourglass on the underside of its abdomen. It is about 3.8-centimetres long with legs extended. The male black widow is only a quarter of this size.

Black Hole

Many scientists believe that when a large star collapses inward from the force of its own weight, a black hole is formed. The density of the collapsed star is so great that light cannot escape, and the star becomes invisible. The black hole has such a strong gravitational pull, it may affect nearby objects such as stars and comets. Scientists closely observe objects that seem to be affected by a strong gravitational pull in an attempt to learn more about black holes.

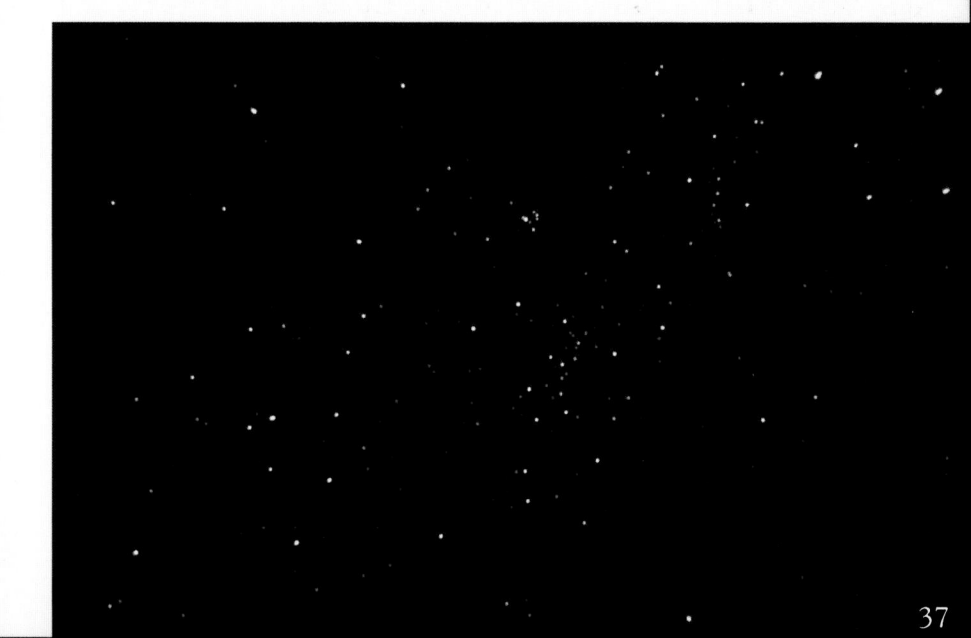

BLACK SAYINGS AND PHRASES

Blackout – a period of darkness caused by a power failure

Black ice – thin, hard, almost transparent ice. This term particularly applies to ice on a road.

In the black – to be in credit at the bank, or to have money. This comes from the business practice of showing accounts with positive balances in black ink.

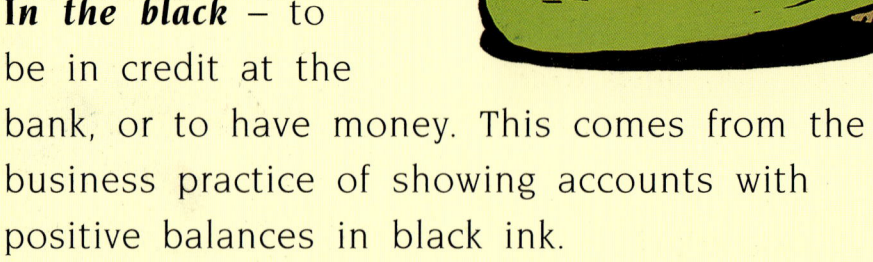

In black and white – to be set down in writing, the paper being white and the ink black

Black light – invisible ultraviolet light

Black

(adj.) 1. having the colour black, like coal (Although we sometimes refer to black as a colour, it really has no colour. Something appears to be black when it absorbs all the light rays that make colour.) **2.** without any light (a black night) **3.** dressed in black **4.** (of tea or coffee) served without milk or cream **(n.) 1.** the colour black **2.** something that is black, such as black clothing (She looks good in black.) **3.** the condition of making a profit (operating in the black)

WHAT IS IT?

Black diamonds are:
1. Coal or truffles
2. Very rare diamonds that are black
3. A type of fish with black diamond-shaped markings
4. Diamond-shaped constellations of very faint stars

COLOURFUL CROSSWORD

The clues for this crossword are on pages 42-43. The answers can all be found somewhere in the book. So, if you can't think of an answer, just keep looking!

Shortland Publications Limited gives its permission to copy the following crossword and clues for classroom use.

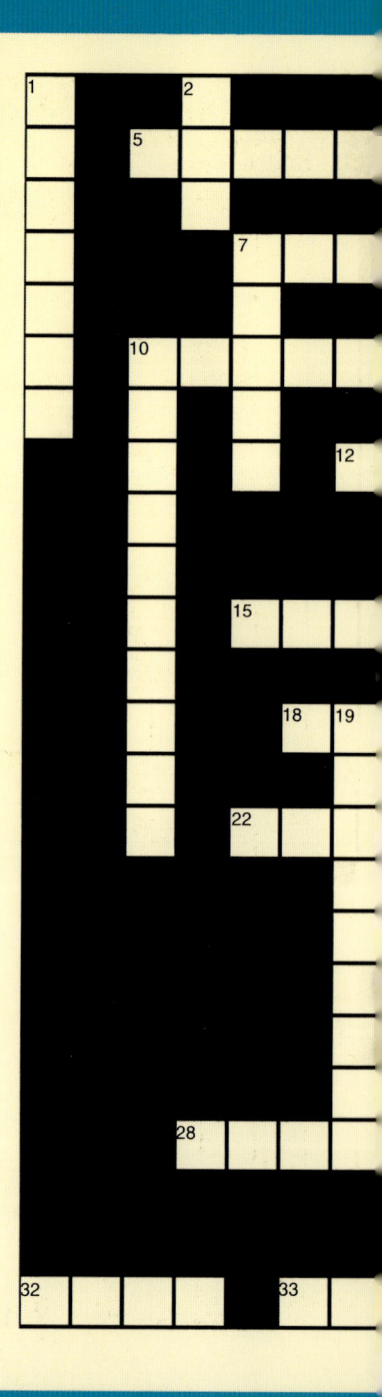

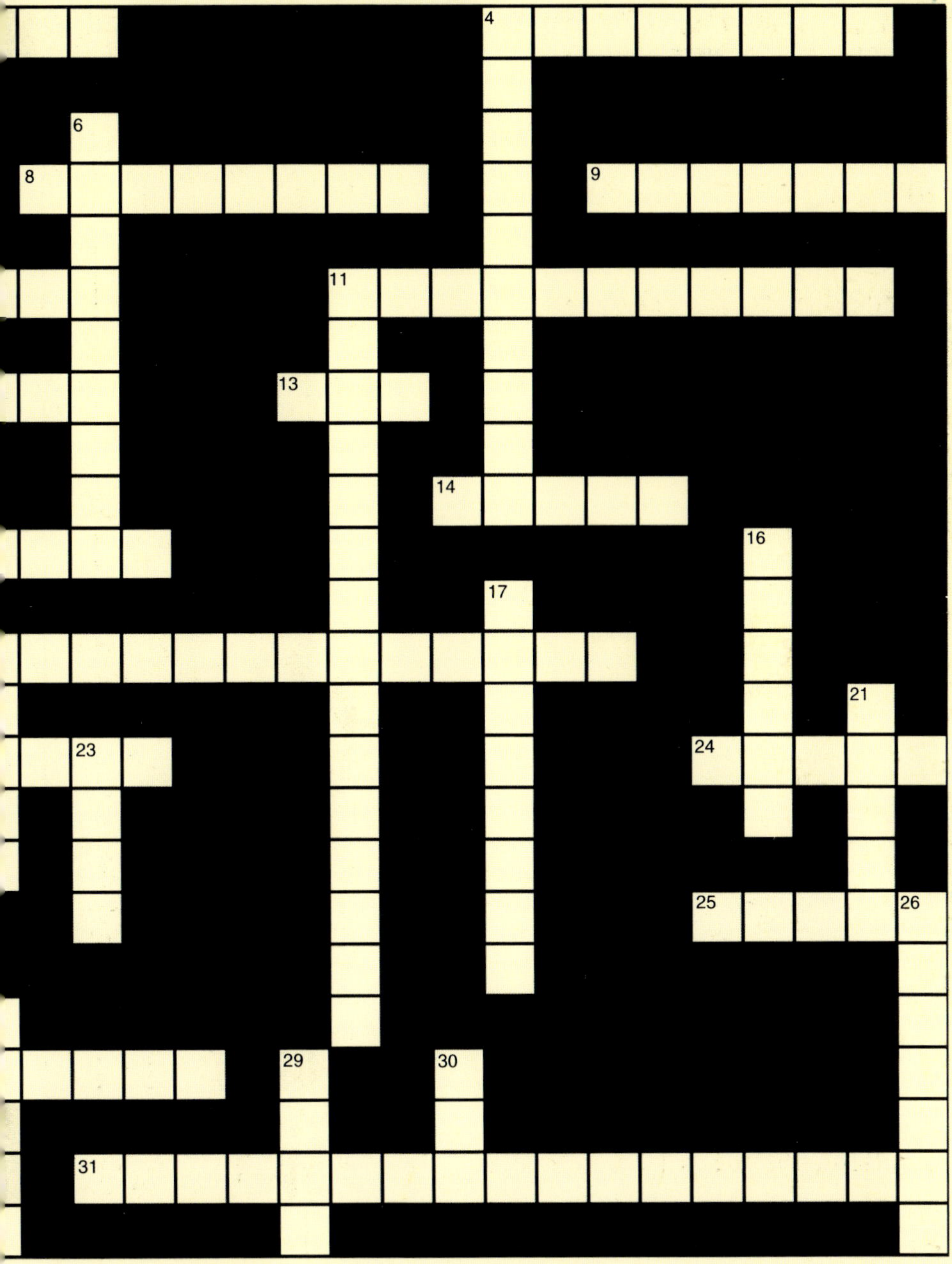
4
6
8
9
11
13
14
16
17
21
23
24
25
26
29
30
31

CROSSWORD CLUES

Across

3. A yellow jacket is a small _ _ _ _ (4 letters)
4. A period of darkness caused by a power failure (8 letters)
5. A traditional form of African-American music (5 letters)
7. The black _ _ _ _ is the most common in North America (4 letters)
8. A saying: Once in a _ _ _ _ _ _ _ _ (8 letters, 2 words)
9. In the past, someone with a greenish complexion was thought to be _ _ _ _ _ _ _ (7 letters)
10. A collapsed star (9 letters, 2 words)
11. The greenhouse _ _ _ _ _ _ _ _ _ _ _ is a pest (11 letters)
12. The blue _ _ _ _ _ is bigger than any dinosaur that ever lived (5 letters)
13. Roll out the _ _ _ carpet for a special visitor (3 letters)
14. The Yellow River is in _ _ _ _ _ (5 letters)
15. One of North America's songbirds (8 letters)
18. The name given to the heating up of Earth's surface as a result of too much carbon dioxide in the atmosphere (16 letters, 2 words)
22. An organization that helps people (8 letters, 2 words)
24. The female black _ _ _ _ _ spider is very dangerous (5 letters)
25. The Huang He is a _ _ _ _ _ in China (5 letters)
28. The official residence of the president of the United States (10 letters, 2 words)
31. Named because of its yellow eyes (17 letters, 3 words)
32. The blue jay is a type of _ _ _ _ (4 letters)
33. The tallest known living _ _ _ _ is a redwood (4 letters)

Down

1. Jealousy is sometimes known as the green-eyed _ _ _ _ _ _ _ (7 letters)
2. A bluebottle _ _ _ (3 letters)
4. A person who works with iron (10 letters)
6. A blue flag with a white panel (9 letters, 2 words)
7. The colour of coal (5 letters)
10. Invisible ultraviolet light (10 letters, 2 words)
11. A snake with white spots along its back (15 letters, 3 words)
16. To be in the black is to be in _ _ _ _ _ _ at the bank (6 letters)
17. There are said to be around 120 million of these animals living on Christmas Island (8 letters, 2 words)
19. Another name for Mars (9 letters, 2 words)
20. The third closest planet to the sun (5 letters)
21. A blacksmith heats iron in a _ _ _ _ _ (5 letters)
23. Many scientists believe that when a large _ _ _ _ collapses inward, a black hole is formed (4 letters)
26. White-water _ _ _ _ _ _ _ is an exciting sport (7 letters)
27. Something appears to be _ _ _ _ _ when it reflects all the light rays that make colour (5 letters)
29. The colour of the green tree _ _ _ _ allows it to hide from enemies and prey (4 letters)
30. Red _ _ _ at night, shepherd's delight (3 letters)

WHAT IS IT? – ANSWERS

A *bluegum* is:

A type of eucalyptus tree native to Australia. The bluegum is the most common eucalyptus tree planted in the United States. It grows very quickly and reaches an enormous size. The bluegum is useful for its oil, gum, and timber.

A *green thumb* is:
Something a person is said to have if they are skilled at growing and tending plants

A *yellowlegs* is:
An American shorebird. There are two species of yellowlegs. They both have black-and-white markings and long yellow legs. In spring, yellowlegs nest in North America. In winter, they can fly as far south as Chile, in South America.

A *red-letter day* is:
A lucky, noteworthy, or memorable day. Originally, the term *red-letter day* referred to a festival marked in red on the calendar.

A *white night* is:
A sleepless night

Black diamonds are:
Coal or truffles. Coal is sometimes referred to as black diamonds because of its importance to industry. Truffles (fungi that grow underground and are considered a delicacy) are also sometimes known as black diamonds because they are very expensive.

Index

black 34-39
black bear 34
black diamonds . . 39, 45
black hole 37
black ice 38
black light 38
blackout 38
blacksmith 35
black widow spider . . 36
blue 4-9
bluebird 4
bluebottle 3, 7
bluegum 9, 44
blue peter 7
blue ribbon 6-7
blues 8
blue whale 5
green 10-15
green-eyed monster . . 14
greenhorn 14
greenhouse 10
greenhouse effect . . . 11
greenhouse grasshopper 10
Greenland 13
green thumb 15, 44
green tree frog 12
green tree python . . . 12
red 22-27
red carpet 26
red crab 22
red cross 24-25
red-letter day . . . 27, 45
red planet 25
red tape 26
redwood 23
white 28-33
white-collar worker . . 32
white elephant 32
White House 28
white night 33, 45
white-out 29
white rhinoceros 30
white-tie affair 32
white water 31
yellow 16-21
yellow-eyed penguin . . 19
yellow fever 20
yellow flag 20
yellow jacket 17
yellowlegs 21, 45
Yellow River 18
Yellowstone Park . . 16-17

From the Author

I have been lucky enough to have lived in a number of countries. On my way to Hong Kong, I sailed across the Red Sea, where the water was the same colour as sea water everywhere. In Kenya, I saw black and white rhinoceros, which were both grey. I flew over the white landscape of Greenland and, in New Zealand, I owned a blue roan cocker spaniel which was black and white.

Thinking about these colourful names gave me the idea for this book, and I was motivated to write it by the hope that I could bring a world of colour to you.

Derek Webb

White Elephants and Yellow Jackets

ISBN 13: 978-0-79-011691-4
ISBN 10: 0-79-011691-X

McGraw Hill Kingscourt

Published by:
McGraw-Hill Education
Shoppenhangers Road, Maidenhead, Berkshire, England, SL6 2QL
Telephone: 44 (0) 1628 502730
Fax: 44 (0) 1628 635895
Website: www.kingscourt.co.uk
Website: www.mcgraw-hill.co.uk

Written by **Derek Webb**
Illustrated by **Fraser Williamson**
Edited by **Frances Bacon**
Designed by **Kristie Rogers**
Photographic research by **Sarah Irvine**

Photography by **Ant Photo Library:** NHPA (P.36); **Auckland Observatory** (Mars, p.25); John Dunlop (night sky, p.37); **Bruce Coleman:** C.B. & D.W. Frith (python, p.12); Wayne Lankinen (p. 4); **Hedgehog House:** Animals Animals/ Michael P. Gadomski (p. 17); Tui De Roy (p.5); J.P. Ferrero (p.22); Mike Langford (p.18); **ICAIR**: Colin Harris (whiteout, p.29); Sarah Irvine: (p.3; p.7); **N.Z. Picture Library:** (grasshopper, pp. 10-11; frog, p.12; p.13; p.19; Red Cross workers, pp. 24-25; p.30; p.34); **Photobank Image Library**: (p.6; greenhouse, pp. 10-11; p.16; p.23; the White House, pp. 28-29; p.31; p.35)

Original Edition © 1997 Shortland Publications
English Reprint Edition © 2010 McGraw-Hill Publishing Company

All rights reserved.

Printed in Hong Kong through Colorcraft Ltd.